HOW TO STUDY THE NEW TESTAMENT

Six Simple Steps

ANTHONY BASH

Lamplighter Books Grand Rapids, Michigan
Zondervan Publishing House

How to Study the New Testament
Copyright © 1988 by Anthony Bash.

First American edition by Zondervan Publishing House, Grand
Rapids, Michigan, with permission from NavPress, England.

Lamplighter Books are published by the
Zondervan Publishing House
1415 Lake Drive, S.E., Grand Rapids, Michigan 49506

Originally published in England under the title *Stepping into
Bible Study*.

Library of Congress Cataloging-in-Publication Data
Bash, Anthony
  [Stepping into Bible study]
  How to Study the New Testament / Anthony Bash.
    p.   cm.
  Reprint. Originally published: Stepping into Bible Study. New
Malden, Surrey, England: NavPress, 1988.
  Includes bibliographical references.
  ISBN 0-310-52951-4
  1. Bible. N.T.–Study. I. Title
BS2530.B29 1990
220′.07–dc20   90-35375
                                                          CIP

All Scripture quotations, unless otherwise noted, are taken from the
Holy Bible, New International Version (North American Edition).
Copyright © 1973, 1978, 1984, by the International Bible Society.
Used by permission of Zondervan Bible Publishers.

All rights reserved. No part of this publication may be reproduced,
stored in a retrieval system, or transmitted in any form or by any
means—electronic, mechanical, photocopy, recording, or any
other—except for brief quotations in printed reviews, without the
prior permission of the publisher.

Printed in the United States of America

90 91 92 93 94 / ML / 10 9 8 7 6 5 4 3 2 1

TO
Garth, Kenny, Gordon and Stewart
whose lives
have so greatly enriched my own

THANKS TO
Steve Wexler, Mick Rolley,
Charles Taylor and John Barclay
for help and advice,
and to the Navigator group at Strathclyde University
for using and commenting on these notes.

CONTENTS

FOREWORD

I am enthusiastic about this book for several reasons...

First, because I am grateful to God for Anthony Bash's ministry in Glasgow with The Navigators, and have observed his great gifts in helping young Christians to study the Bible.

Secondly, because there is a great need for a basic introduction to Bible Study, which takes nothing for granted except a willingness to commit oneself to the task. I wish such a book had been available years ago.

Thirdly, because the book itself is so good. I know nothing quite like it. It combines excellent content with a lucidity of style which makes it easy and attractive to read.

I have no doubt that it will be widely used for years to come, to the lasting benefit of many, and for their growth in the knowledge of God.

Eric J. Alexander

INTRODUCTION

Why Study Scripture?
Bible study is hard work. It takes time and discipline. So why do it? Here are five reasons...

<u>The Bible is From God</u>
2 Timothy 3:16 says that all Scripture is "inspired," or "God-breathed."

This means that the Bible is breathed out by God. Its words are God's words, its thoughts are God's thoughts. The words on the page come from God's mouth and vocal chords.

<u>The Bible is About God</u>
God cannot be known or understood unless He reveals Himself to us. He cannot be deduced or hypothesized. Certainty and knowledge about His being and character can only come if He tells us who He is. The Bible is our primary source of that knowledge. Every page of the Bible is about God.

<u>The Bible Equips Us to Serve God</u>
Scripture sets out God's will for our lives and so enables us to make a proper response of worship, love and obedi-

ence to Him. It also equips us for personal ministry
(2 Timothy 3:16) and every good work (2 Timothy 3:17).

The Bible Can Change Us
If we will put into practice what the Bible teaches, God
promises to transform us increasingly into His likeness
(2 Corinthians 3:18 and Romans 12:1,2).

Others Have Studied the Bible
Scripture contains examples of many who studied and
knew God's word, and who as a result were greatly
blessed:

- Daniel "set [his] mind to gain understanding and to
    humble [himself] before [his] God" (Daniel 10:12).
- Ezra "devoted himself to the study and observ-
    ance of the Law of the Lord, and to teach its
    decrees and laws" (Ezra 7:10).
- A glance at the Gospels shows Jesus' intimate know-
    ledge and thorough understanding of the Old
    Testament.
- In Acts 17:11 Luke records approvingly how the
    Bereans "examined the Scriptures every day to see if
    what Paul said was true."

What is Bible Study?
One dictionary gives this definition of the word "study":
"the devotion of time to the acquisition of information;
a careful examination or observation of something."

This is a good starting point for a definition of Bible
study. In other words, in studying the Bible, we devote
time to acquiring understanding about the Bible, and to
examining carefully what it says.

But there is more to it than that. True Bible study is not
just a matter of acquiring information and knowledge: it

should affect not only the mind, but also the heart and will, and should lead to obedience to and worship of God. Besides learning *about* the Bible, we should also expect to see our day-to-day living changed *by* the Bible.

A good definition of Bible study might therefore be: "the prayerful application of the mind to developing a greater understanding of what the Bible teaches, in order to obey it, and thereby be transformed more into the image of Christ."

What Will Happen?

If you follow the Six Steps to Studying the Letters (Part 1) and the Six Steps to Studying the Gospels (Part 2), you will learn the basic methods of New Testament Bible study, methods which you will then be able to apply to any part of Scripture.

> *"My son, if you accept my words*
> *and store up my commands within you,*
> *turning your ear to wisdom*
> *and applying your heart to understanding,*
> *and if you call out for insight*
> *and cry aloud for understanding,*
> *and if you look for it as for silver*
> *and search for it as for hidden treasure,*
> *then you will understand the fear of the Lord*
> *and find the knowledge of God.*
> *For the Lord gives wisdom,*
> *and from His mouth come knowledge and*
> *understanding."*
> (Proverbs 2:1-6)

This book has been written with the prayer that through our study of the Scriptures God would help us to fear and know Him, and give us wisdom, knowledge and understanding so that we can worship and serve Him.

BEFORE YOU START...

What is This Book About?

As you study any New Testament book chapter by chapter, you progress from Step to Step. And so, chapter by chapter, Step by Step, week by week, you develop in your knowledge and love of Scripture -- and put its teaching into practice.

These notes are designed primarily for use in home groups whose members are willing to spend some time preparing each study before meeting together; but they can also be used by individuals studying alone.

One member of the group should act as leader, and ideally this person should lead the group every time the group meets. Notes on leading are given at the end of the book.

What Do I Need?

1. A notebook to write down your thoughts and comments. That means you will have a record of what you have learned, which you will be able to refer to in the future.

2. A copy of the Bible. A modern, easy-to-understand

translation of the Bible is preferable. The *New International Version* (published by Zondervan) is widely used and is recommended. Other translations are useful for reference.

3. Although reference books are not absolutely necessary, they can be very helpful. Two good commentaries are *The Eerdmans Bible Commentary* (Eerdmans) and *The Bible Knowledge Commentary* (Victor). Also useful is *The New Bible Dictionary* (Tyndale). Other reference books are recommended in the course of this book.

How Do I Get Down to Studying?

You will find it a help to plan a regular study time into your schedule. Pick a time of the week when you are reasonably alert, and find a quiet room, away from distractions. At first you may not be able to concentrate for very long. However you will find that the more you study, the better you become at it, and the longer you can concentrate. Regular Bible study takes discipline and commitment, and it is wise to make it a matter of prayer.

PART 1

SIX STEPS
TO
STUDYING
THE
NEW TESTAMENT
LETTERS

PREFACE

What are the Letters?

The New Testament letters (often called "epistles") consist of thirteen letters from the Apostle Paul, two from the Apostle Peter, one called The Letter to the Hebrews (which is anonymous, but is traditionally regarded as by Paul), three from the Apostle John, one from Jude, and one from James. (The Letter to the Hebrews and the First Letter of John may not in fact be letters at all, although for our purposes they can be studied as if they were.)

The Book of Revelation is a letter, but should be studied using a combination of the suggestions for studying the letters (Part 1) and those for studying the Gospels (Part 2). Revelation is a difficult book and is not recommended for the new Bible student.

Why Study the Letters?

The letters are:

1. An explanation and exploration of the *meaning* of the life, ministry, death and resurrection of Jesus Christ;

2. A study of the moral and ethical *implications* of the life, ministry, death and resurrection of Jesus Christ;

3. Practical *instruction* for Christians in daily living and in church life and leadership.

What Do I Do?

Part 1 of this book contains six Steps to studying the New Testament letters. It has been written with the assumption that the first book you intend to study has at least four chapters.

Start with Step 1. This Step will enable you to study the background of a letter and to identify some of its major themes and emphases.

Follow Step 2 to study chapter one of the letter, Step 3 to study chapter two, Step 4 with chapter three, and Step 5 with chapter four.

When you have studied all the chapters of the letter, proceed to Step 6. This Step will help you to see the letter as a whole, and to draw together the lessons you have learned.

By the time you have completed Step 6, you will have learned a method of Bible study which you can use with any New Testament letter.

Where Do I Begin?

It may be wiser to begin with some of the shorter, easier-to-understand New Testament letters, such as Ephesians, Colossians and Philippians. 1 Thessalonians is also fairly straightforward, as are 1 and 2 Timothy.

STEP 1
Preliminary and Background Study

Introduction
In Step 1, we consider how to study the background of a New Testament letter, and how to get a broad picture of what it is about. Our objective is to establish the historical and cultural setting of a letter and to identify its major themes and emphases, as a prelude to a detailed study of its contents.

Method of Study
1. Read the letter through at least three times, preferably in more than one translation.

2. With the aid of a commentary, Bible handbook or New Testament introduction, try to discover the answers to the following questions...
   - Who wrote the letter? – *Paul.*
   - To whom was the letter written?
   - When was the letter written? *While Paul was in Pris...*
   - What is the historical setting of the letter? -

3. Answer the following questions...
   - What is the major emphasis of the letter?
   - What are some of the recurring ideas?
   - What subjects does the author deal with?

- Are there any often recurring words or phrases?
- Why do you think the letter was written?
- What was the author trying to accomplish?
- What specific problems was the writer dealing with?

**Don't avoid
reference material**

4. <u>Optional Question</u> Write an outline of the letter. These suggestions may help you...
    - What are the broad sections into which the letter falls?
    - Give each of the sections a heading.
    - Write brief notes on each of the sections.
(An example of an outline prepared according to these three stages is given an the end of this Step.)

5. Can you think of a title for the whole book? The title should briefly encapsulate the theme and teaching of the book. (A suggestion for Philippians might be "Christian Joy and Progress," and for Galatians "Gospel, Faith and Law.")

6. Can you see any modern parallels with the subjects dealt with in the letter?

7. Is there any truth from the letter which you think God is asking you to put into practice? What should you do?

Part of an Outline of Galatians

1:1-5   Introduction
1:1   From Paul
1:2   To the church in Galatia
1:3-5   Blessing

1:6-2:21   Only One Gospel
1:6-7   The church following another gospel
1:8-9   There is only one gospel
1:10   Paul not seeking to please his audience with the gospel he preached
1:11-17   The gospel given by revelation
1:18-2:10   The gospel preached by Paul confirmed by others
2:11-21   Paul opposed Peter when he misunderstood the gospel

                 . . .

STEP 2
Outline and
Verse-by-Verse
Meditation

Introduction

You should use this Step to help you consider the first chapter of the letter you are studying.

In this study, we will consider how to meditate on a passage of Scripture. But before meditating, it is helpful to have an overall picture or outline of the passage. This will help us to see how the individual verses fit into the passage as a whole.

Writing an Outline

An outline is intended to give a summary of the content and main thrust of a chapter. Writing one is not just an academic exercise; it should help you to understand and remember the structure and meaning of a chapter. The following suggestions may help you prepare an outline...

1. Read the chapter through at least three times.

2. Group the verses together into paragraphs. Remember that the section divisions and titles given in your Bible are not part of the original text (nor, often, are the paragraph divisions), so you may overlook them in order to arrive at your own division of the chapter.

3. Give each of your paragraphs a brief descriptive title (e.g. "Spiritual Armor" for Ephesians 6:10-20).

4. Make brief notes of the content of each paragraph.

(If you have already prepared an outline of the chapter in Step 1, re read your outline, and make amendments in the light of your further study.)

Verse-by-Verse Meditation

Verse-by-verse meditation helps us focus on what a passage both says and means. Meditation on Scripture is not day-dreaming or mystical vacuousness; it should be prayerful and deliberate thought about the content, meaning and application of a certain passage. It should lead us to a deeper understanding of Scripture and to worship and obedience.

Select a minimum of six consecutive verses from the chapter. Use the following questions to help you reflect on them. Not all the questions will be relevant to the verses you are considering. As you reflect, write down your thoughts and comments.

Context
- What goes before? What follows?
- Are there any link words (e.g. "for," "therefore")?
- Are there any references to other parts of the letter?

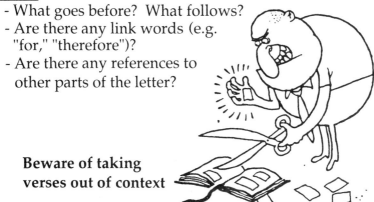

Beware of taking verses out of context

Clarification
- What did the author mean?
- Are there any words or phrases I do not understand? What could they mean?
- How would I put the verse in my own words?

Questions
- What do I still not understand?
- What should I study further?

Comment
- What particularly stands out to me?
- How can I put it into practice in the next few days?

Commitment
- What truth is conveyed by this teaching?
- How can I put it into practice?

Conclusions
- How does this section fit into the rest of the chapter?
- In the light of my meditation, do I want to amend my outline?

STEP 3
Title and Key Verse

Introduction
This Step will help us to find a title and key verse for a chapter. Once again, we will produce an outline for the chapter and spend some time doing a verse-by-verse meditation on a section of it.

You should follow this Step as you consider the second chapter of the letter you are studying.

Preliminary
Using the methods described in Step 2, prepare an outline of the chapter and meditate on a minimum of six consecutive verses.

Title
Using your outline to assist you...
- What is the chapter about?
- What themes occur in the chapter?
- What do you think is the main thing the writer is saying in this chapter?

Having answered these questions, think of a title for the chapter. Your title should summarize the chapter briefly and memorably. An example of such a title might be: "To Marry or Not to Marry?" for 1 Corinthians 7, or "Heroes of Faith" for Hebrews 11.

Key Verse
Is there a verse which summarizes what the chapter is saying? Are there perhaps two such verses? It/they should relate to your title and be consistent with your outline. This/these will be your key verse(s).

Finally . . .
Look over your Bible study again. Do you want to make any changes to your outline, title or choice of a key verse? If so, make the alterations.

What do you think God is asking you to put into practice in the next few days?

STEP 4
Putting the Bible into Practice

Introduction
How can we put into practice the teaching and principles
which we find through our study of the Bible? In this
Step, we consider how to make a prayerful and practical
response to Scripture. Such a response is often known as
an "application."

Use this Step with the third chapter of the letter you are
studying.

Applications
The application part of our Bible study is a practical way
of helping us obey God and His Word. An application is
not something we prepare simply to please our Bible
study group leader, but a willing response of obedience to
God. It is relatively easy to think one up, but such an
application may not reflect what God is really asking you
to do.

Begin by prayer, and ask God to show you what He is
asking you to do. In Psalm 139:23-24 David prayed,
  "Search me, O God, and know my heart;
  test me and know my anxious thoughts.

See if there is any offensive way in me,
and lead me in the way everlasting."
Why not make David's words your own?

Continue to pray while you are studying. Ask God to give you insight into the way you are, into the way you should be, and how He wants you to get from one to the other! You should be open to God and to what He wants you to be -- it is not a good idea to have "closed" areas which you do not allow God to deal with! If we really do want to become people who live for Christ, then we will eagerly consider how to apply the Word to our lives.

Write down what you think God is asking you to do. First state the need, next write what you propose to do about it, and finally come up with some sort of a review procedure -- some way of checking that you do what you have decided to do (e.g. "Ask Bob to make sure I do this"). In short, an application should be practical, possible and personal.

Consider the following examples of applications. Do you think they are satisfactory? Why or why not?

1. "I have been challenged recently by Hebrews 10.25 to 'encourage' my friends. I know that Richard and Jim are discouraged at present. I will ring them up to invite each of them over for coffee. Before they come, I will pray and ask God to help me to be sensitive to their needs and to be an encouragement to them."

2. "Paul says somewhere that we must speak the truth with one another. A lot of little things I have been saying recently have been bothering me. I really must do something about this."

When your Bible study group meets, you might discuss whether you have managed to put into practice the applications you shared at your previous meeting.

Bible Study
Following the methods previously given...
- Prepare an outline of the chapter.
- Meditate on a minimum of six consecutive verses.
- Suggest a title and key verse for the chapter.
- Write down your application. Is it practical, personal and possible?

And Then . . .
Review your application daily and ask God to help you to put it into practice. You may find it helpful to ask a friend to pray for you and help monitor your progress.

STEP 5
Cross-Referencing

Introduction
In this Step we will learn how to cross-reference one passage of Scripture with others.

You should use this Step to help you to consider the fourth chapter of the letter you are studying.

What is Cross-Referencing?
As you prepare your Bible study, you will constantly come across themes which are explained more fully in other parts of the Bible. To refer passages to other parts of the Bible is to "cross-reference" them. In other words, cross-referencing is comparing Scripture with Scripture. This is absolutely essential if our Bible study is to be thorough, accurate and balanced.

For example, if you were studying Hebrews 7, you would read that Christ is "a high priest after the order of Melchizedek" (verses 11 and 17). If you wanted to understand better the nature Christ's priesthood, you might want to cross-reference that phrase with Old Testament passages which refer to the high priest or to Melchizedek.

Similarly in Hebrews 7:25 you would see that Christ

"saves those who draw near to him." You might want to cross-reference that phrase with other parts of the Bible that explain how and why Jesus saves people.

Cross-referencing can be fun

How Do I Find Cross-References?
Your Bible may give cross-references in its center columns or at the foot of the page. If not, there is no easy or simple method of cross-referencing; the greater your knowledge of the Bible, the easier will be your task. The following suggestions and guidelines may help. Ask yourself,

1. "What other portions of Scripture do I know which clarify this passage? What do I learn from them that influences my understanding of the passage I am studying?" (Cross-references given in your Bible may help here too).

2. "Does what I learn here appear to be contradicted by other parts of Scripture?" If so, how might these passages be reconciled?

A Concordance (see page 57) and other Bible reference books will also help you to find cross-references.

Bible Study

Following the methods previously given...

1. Prepare an outline of the chapter,
2. Meditate on a minimum of six consecutive verses,
3. Suggest a title for the chapter and a key verse,
4. Find cross-references for one of the chapter's major themes,
5. Write out your application.

What Next?

If the letter you are studying has more than four chapters, continue to study its remaining chapters following the principles of study given above. (You may also like to read the Three Suggestions... on pages 57-63.)

After you have studied the last chapter of the letter, go on to Step 6.

STEP 6
Concluding Study

Introduction
You should follow this Step after you have completed the last chapter of the letter you are studying. This Step aims to help us to see the letter as a whole.

Method of Study
1. <u>Review</u> Re-read the letter and all your notes on it.

2. <u>Book Title</u> Re-consider your chapter outlines and chapter titles. Can you see any common themes running through them? Can you think of one title for the letter which would summarize its contents? That will be your book title.

3. <u>Major Doctrines and Teaching</u> What are the major doctrines and teachings in the letter? What have you learned about them?

4. <u>Special Words or Phrases</u> Does the letter contain any special words or phrases? What is their significance? What have you learned about them?

5. <u>Key Verse or Passage</u> Is there one verse or passage which sums up the teaching and thrust of the letter?

That verse or passage should relate to your letter title and your statement of the major themes and doctrines.

6. <u>Historical Background</u> How does the teaching of the letter meet the needs or problems which the author faced when he wrote the letter?

7. <u>Personal Lessons</u> What has God been teaching you through your study of the letter? What sins has He revealed? What have you done about them? Did you make any applications that you still haven't carried out?

PART 2

SIX STEPS
TO STUDYING
THE GOSPELS

PREFACE

Why Study the Gospels?
The Gospels are biographical, recording the life, work, death and resurrection of Jesus Christ. And yet much of Christ's life is omitted. Broadly speaking, the focus of the Gospels is on the last three years of Christ's life, and a special emphasis is put on His death and the days immediately before. So even within that three-year period, the writers were highly selective in what they recorded.

Why then should we study them?

1. The Gospels tell us about Jesus Christ -- the source and center of our faith, and the reason for it.

2. The writers wrote because they wanted their readers to have a proper understanding of who Jesus Christ was and therefore who, in His resurrected life, He still is. In other words, they wanted us to understand and know Him as a Person.

3. Jesus Christ is our great example, whom the Bible tells us we are to imitate in character and action.

4. The Gospels contain the fullest record of Jesus Christ's

teaching, teaching we ourselves are to practise and pass on to others.

These notes will help you to study any Gospel chapter by chapter, to consider it in relation to the other Gospels, and to let its truths influence your life and service for Christ. Although not a Gospel, the Book of Acts can also be studied using the Steps in this section (but for information on harmonizing it, see the note on Acts in Step 4).

What Do I Do?

The first two Steps will help you to understand the background of a Gospel, to analyse its structure and to begin to see it as a whole.

These two Steps are probably the longest studies in the whole of this book, and those new to Bible study may feel daunted by what they are asked to do. You may prefer to omit Step 1 and Step 2 and to rely on what commentators say about the background, structure and content of the Gospel.

Steps 3, 4 and 5 will help you to study the individual chapters of the Gospel. So, follow Step 3 to study chapter 1, Step 4 with chapter 2 and Step 5 with chapter 3. Continue to study the remaining chapters in the Gospel following the instructions in Step 5.

Follow Step 6 after you have studied the last chapter of the Gospel. You may wish to use the same Step to study more than one Bible chapter. By all means do so; in fact, you should not go on to a new Step until you feel that you have begun to master the Step you are working on.

Which Gospel Should I Study First?

It does not make a great deal of difference. Start with

whichever you like -- you may want to remember that Mark is the shortest!

How Long Should I Spend Studying Each Chapter?

As long as you want! There is no minimum or maximum time. Most people take anything from an hour and a half upwards to complete one chapter. But Step 1 and Step 2 will take the longest time to complete, because in each you are asked to read a complete Gospel at least once.

Don't get bogged down over details

STEP 1
Preliminary and
Background Study

Introduction
In this Step we consider how to study the background of a
Gospel, and how to get a broad picture of its contents. To
do this, we will identify some of the themes of the Gospel, and consider whether the writer wishes to highlight
any specific aspects of Christ's life and ministry.

This study will take about twice as long to complete as
most of the rest in this book. If you are new to Bible
study you may wish to omit Step 1 and Step 2.

Method of Study
1. <u>Optional Question</u> Read the Gospel through at least
   once at the same speed at which you would read any
   other book (such as a novel). As you read, write down
   what you specially notice in the Gospel. What impres-
   sions do you have of the Gospel as a whole?

2. Read through the Gospel at least once slowly and
   make notes on the following questions:

   a. Are we told who wrote the Gospel? (The title of the
      Gospel given in your Bible is not part of the original

text.) If not, are there clues in the text as to who the author may be?

b. Does the writer indicate why he wrote? If not, what do you think the writer wanted his readers to learn?

c. Are there any recurring emphases or themes? What do you think is their significance?

d. Using a Bible Atlas (or your Bible if it has maps), locate the places mentioned in the Gospel. (You may want to draw a simple map in your notebook and mark the places on it.)

e. What things have you learned about Jesus Christ and about Christian living? How could you begin to put this into practice?

STEP 2
Writing an Outline
of a Gospel

Introduction

In this Step we will first learn how to write an outline of
a Gospel, and then use the outline to help us better
understand the Gospel as a whole.

As in the case of Step 1, this study will take about twice as
long to complete as most of the rest in this book. If you
are new to Bible study, you may wish to omit this Step.

Method of Study

1. Read the Gospel through slowly and, as you do so,
   make a note of the broad sections into which it falls.
   These sections may, for example, describe Christ's
   work and ministry in a particular place (e.g. His ministry in Judea in Matthew 19:1-20:16) or His discussions
   and confrontations with religious figures (e.g. John
   6:25-8:59). There are no necessarily "correct" ways of
   dividing up the sections.

2. Give each of the sections a heading.

3. Write brief notes on the contents of each of these
   sections.

(An example of an outline prepared according to these three stages is given at the end of this Step.)

4. Consider the outline you have prepared.
   a. How has it helped you to understand the Gospel better?
   b. What have you learned about Jesus Christ or about Christian life and ministry?
   c. Are there any truths from your study which you should begin to put into practice? What should you do?

Part of an Outline of Mark's Gospel

1:1-1:13	<u>Preparation for Ministry</u>
1:1	Introduction
1:2-11	John the Baptist and Jesus
1:2-8	John and his ministry
1:9-11	Jesus' own baptism
1:12,13	Jesus' temptations
1:14-7:23	<u>Ministry in Galilee</u>
1:14,15	Jesus' message
1:16-20	Calls of Simon, Andrew, James, John
1:28-34	Healings at Capernaum
1:35-38	Morning prayer
1:39	Ministry throughout Galilee
1:40-45	Healing of leper
2:1-12	Healing of paralytic at Capernaum
2:13-17	Call of Levi and visit to Levi's house
2:18-27	Discussion with Pharisees: fasts, sabbaths
3:1-6	Healing of man with withered hand
3:7-9	Spread of Jesus' fame
3:10-12	Healings and exorcisms
3:13-19	Call of the Twelve
	. . .

STEP 3
Outlining and Meditating on a Chapter

Introduction
You are now ready to begin studying the Gospel's contents in more detail.

Use this Step with the first chapter of the Gospel you are studying. (Remember though, that the verse and chapter divisions in your Bible are not part of the original text, and so you may prefer to study slightly more or less than a chapter.)

This Step will show how to prepare an outline of the chapter. The purpose of preparing an outline is to help fix the chapter in our minds and to clarify its contents. We will also learn how to meditate on the chapter.

Outlining the Chapter
1. Slowly and prayerfully read the chapter you are studying at least three times.

2. Note down the broad sections into which the chapter falls and give each section a title.

3. Make short notes on the contents of each section.

(An example of an outline of a chapter prepared according to these three stages is given at the end of this Step.)

4. If you did Step 2, re-read your outline of the whole Gospel, and try to understand the chapter you are studying in the context of the rest of the Gospel.

Meditating on the Chapter
Meditation on Scripture is not day-dreaming in front of a Bible or sitting in a certain position with a blank mind! It is prayerfully reflecting on a passage so that we can understand its meaning better, and apply its truths to our lives.

Choose a section of at least six verses, and meditate on each verse using the method below.

1. Begin with prayer. Ask God to give you insight and help you apply truths from the chapter to your own life.

2. Ask yourself what each verse tells you about Jesus Christ and about His life and ministry. Reflect on what He said and did, how He reacted, how He loved and served people, and what this tells you of who He is.

3. What did Christ teach in this chapter? Are you obeying it? What should you do or not do?

4. How did others react to Christ? What can we learn from their reactions?

5. What is God asking you to put into practice? Take practical steps to obey Him by writing down...

a. what God is asking you to do,
b. how you have fallen short,
c. what you intend to do,
d. how you intend to do it
-- think of some practical
steps to put your intentions
into effect.

6. Thank God for what you have
learned. Take some time to worship
and praise Him, and ask Him to help you put into
practice what you have learned.

Example of an Outline of Mark 5

1. <u>The Gerasene Demoniac</u>
5:1	- The journey across the sea
5:2-5	- The demoniac's pitiful condition
5:6,7	- The demoniac's response to Jesus
5:8,9	- Jesus' response to the demoniac
5:10-13	- Jesus exorcises the demoniac

2. <u>Responses to the Miracle</u>
5:14	- The herdsmen
5:15-17	- The people
5:18	- The former demoniac
5:19,20	- Jesus' commission to the demoniac

3. <u>Request to Heal Jairus' Daughter</u>
   | 5:21-23 | - Jairus requests Jesus to heal his dying daughter |
   | 5:24a | - Jesus agrees |

4. <u>Interruption by the Woman with Bleeding</u>
   5:24b-29 - Woman in crowd healed of bleeding

5:30-32 - Jesus wants to know who was healed
5:33,34 - The woman identifies herself and speaks
            to Jesus

5. <u>Jairus' Daughter Raised</u>
   5:35   - News given that Jairus' daughter had died
   5:36   - Jesus' response to the news
   5:37-43 - Jesus raises the girl from the dead

STEP 4
Harmonizing
the Gospels

Introduction

Use this Step with the second chapter of the Gospel you are studying.

Each of the Gospels emphasizes different aspects of Jesus' life and ministry. The Gospels are four accounts of the same life, but written with different purposes and told from different viewpoints. It can be a great help for us to identify the writer's specific interest and purpose in writing.

Suppose you read a report in a newspaper about a football game.   The writer of the report almost certainly intended to write an accurate account of what took place, but had to be selective in what he said. Another writer reporting the same event in a different newspaper will report the event differently, including additional material and omitting other material. Both will have written about the same event, but the reports will be different.

Similarly, if yet another writer wanted to write an account of the football game but had not been present when the game was played, he would draw on existing newspaper reports, and might also interview some of the players and spectators.

It is not that one of these reports is true, and the others false. They are different; and by reading them together you would arrive at a fuller understanding of what actually happened. And you might also get a picture of the interests and intentions of the individual reporters.

So it is with the Gospel accounts. There are both differences and similarities between them. The differences may arise because of the writers' different styles, knowledge, and approaches. They may also arise because the writers consulted other records as they wrote.

Consequently, by comparing one Gospel with another you may arrive at a better understanding of the writers' aims and purposes. And if you combine one account with another, you may obtain a fuller statement of what actually took place.

What we can say however (unlike in the case of a newspaper reporter) is that each Gospel writer wrote what he did under the hand of God, that it is Scripture and therefore "God-breathed." Whether a Gospel is considered individually or with the others, it is God's word to us, and can profitably be studied (2 Timothy 3:16,17).

Use of a Gospel Harmony
Here are two ways in which you can find out whether the contents of a chapter of one Gospel is referred to in other Gospels...

1. Your Bible may contain cross-references (that is, references to other parts of the Bible which are relevant to the portion being read). These cross-references may be to a specific word or phrase; in the case of the Gospels, they very often refer also to an account of the same event recorded in another Gospel. By looking up these parallel passages, you can begin to compare one Gospel with another.

Comparison

2. You may wish also to consult a Gospel "Harmony." This is a book which sets out all four Gospels in parallel columns. (Some Gospel Harmonies are only of the "Synoptic" Gospels, that is, Matthew, Mark and Luke.) Thus you can see at a glance what each Gospel omits and includes, and how the same events are treated differently. Large reference libraries often have a Gospel Harmony.

(*Note on the Book of Acts* If you are studying the Book of Acts you can harmonize it by examining the letters that relate to the events recorded in the book: for example, 1 Corinthians sheds light on Paul's trip to Corinth in Acts 18.)

Method of Study
1. Write an outline of the chapter, and meditate on part of it, following the instructions in Step 3. Consider what you believe God is asking you to put into practice.

2. Using a Bible with cross-references or a Gospel Har-

mony (or by hard work, simply looking through the other Gospels), note down accounts in the other gospels that parallel what you are studying.

a. What is omitted? What is additional?
b. Do the other accounts help you better understand the passage you are studying? If so, how?
c. Do the omissions and/or additions help you to understand the writer's purposes and intentions? If so, how?

3. Reconsider what you believe God is asking you to put into practice. Write it down. Then do it!

Contrast

STEP 5
Relating a Chapter
to the Rest of Scripture

Introduction

Use this Step with the third chapter of the Gospel you are studying. Scripture is written by men, but inspired by God. It all comes from the same source, the same mind, and the same Person -- God Himself.

It follows that one portion of Scripture can elaborate or explain another, and can be better understood in the context of other parts of Scripture.

The mature Bible student will therefore seek to understand the place of the passage he is studying within biblical revelation as a whole. This Step discusses some ways of doing that.

Relating a Chapter to Other Scriptures

There is no easy or quick method of relating the passage you are studying to the rest of Scripture. The greater your knowledge of the Bible, the easier will be your task.

The questions below may help you to begin to do this. Ask yourself,

1. "Do I know any other passages which explain or relate

to what this passage is saying? How do they influence my understanding of this passage?"

2. "How is what I learn of Jesus Christ, His ministry and teaching modelled or taught elsewhere in Scripture?"

3. "Does what I learn here appear to be contradicted by other parts of Scripture?" If so, how might these passages be reconciled?

4. Look up the cross-references given in your Bible. Do they help you to understand the passage you are studying? If so, how?

5. <u>For advanced Bible students</u> A Concordance and an Expository Dictionary will help you to relate what you are studying to the rest of Scripture; read Suggestion 1 and Suggestion 2 on pages 57-61.

Method of Study
1. Following the instructions in Step 3, write an outline of the chapter and meditate on it (or part of it).

2. Using the cross-references in your Bible or a Gospel Harmony, harmonize the chapter following the instructions in Step 4.

3. As set out above, relate at least one truth in the chapter you are studying to the wider teaching of Scripture.

4. Reconsider what you believe God is asking you to put into practice -- you will have considered this already when meditating on the chapter. Should you now add to or amend what you have written?

Further Study in the Rest of the Gospel
Continue to study the remaining chapters of the Gospel

using this Step. It will be hard work but, as you will have already discovered, very rewarding. You may like to read Suggestion 3 on page 62 for more help in developing and deepening your Bible study.

STEP 6
Concluding Study

Introduction
Follow this Step after you have completed the last chapter of the Gospel you are studying.

This Step aims to help you to see the Gospel as a whole, after your study of its individual chapters.

Method of Study
1. Re-read the Gospel and all your notes on it. In the light of your study of the whole Gospel, do you wish to amend the outline you prepared in Step 2?

2. What are the major themes and emphases of the Gospel?

3. What specific aspects of Christ's life and ministry stand out to you?

4. What major truths do you think the Gospel writer was seeking to teach?

5. What lessons have you learned through your study? How has your understanding deepened?

6. What do you think is the greatest lesson to you from your study?

7. Look over the various things that God been asking you to put into practice in your studies. Can you see any common elements to what God has been saying to you? Can you summarize the lessons?

8. How can you carry on obeying what God has been saying to you?

PART 3

THREE SUGGESTIONS FOR DEEPENING YOUR BIBLE STUDY

SUGGESTION 1
Using a Concordance

Introduction
As you study the Scriptures, you will come across words which you know are significant and occur elsewhere in the Bible. Examining the other occurrences of a word could give you a much better understanding of its meaning. If you want to do this, a concordance is an essential reference book.

What is a Concordance?
A concordance is a book which lists the Bible references to words. So if, for example, you look up the word "faith" in a concordance, you find a list of all the occurrences of that word.

Types of Concordance
The two most important types of concordances are exhaustive and analytical. Exhaustive concordances, such as Strong's and *The NIV Exhaustive Concordance*, list every occurrence of every word in the Bible. The words are listed in the order in which they occur in Scripture.

Some exhaustive concordances also give help with the

Hebrew and Greek words behind the English translation. A word in the original language may be translated in a number of different ways in English. The Greek word "doxa," for example, is translated "dignity," "glory," "honour," "praise," and "worship" in different parts of one Bible version. Strong's and *The NIV Exhaustive Concordance* get over this difficulty by pointing out which Hebrew or Greek word is behind the translation of each English word.

An analytical concordance, such as Young's, groups words together on the basis of the Hebrew or Greek word behind the English translation. This type of concordance is useful because several different Greek words may be translated into the same English word. The word "love," for example, may be used to translate the Hebrew word "aheb" and the Greek words "agapaō" and "phileō." By consulting an analytical concordance, you can immediately tell which Hebrew or Greek word is behind each translation of the word "love."

How to Use a Concordance
The concordance you use should match the translation you prefer. The concordances edited by Strong and Young are based on the King James Version of the Bible. *The NIV Exhaustive Concordance* is based on the *New International Version*.

Suppose, for example, you wanted to use a concordance to study the word "love" as it occurs in a certain passage in the New Testament. This is how you would do it. . .

If you have a copy of Strong's or *The NIV Exhaustive Concordance*, find the entry under "love" for the verse you are studying. There will be a number on the right-hand side. Look up that number in the Greek-English dictionary at the back of the concordance, and you will find the original Greek word and various ways that Greek word is translated into English. You can then look up these translations in the main body of the concordance.

If you have a copy of Young's concordance, find the entry under "love" for the word you are studying. The original Greek word will appear in anglicized form at the head of the column. Look up that anglicized word in the New Testament Lexicon at the back of the concordance. There you will find listed every English translation of the Greek word. These words can then be studied using the concordance.

SUGGESTION 2
Using an Expository Dictionary

Introduction

As you prepare your Bible study, you are likely to come across words which you would like to study in greater detail. You may be aware that these are words which have a special or unusual meaning in the Bible. An Expository Dictionary may help you to understand these words better.

An Expository Dictionary

An Expository Dictionary is a dictionary of Bible words which defines them according to their biblical meaning. The most well-known such dictionary is *An Expository Dictionary of Bible Words* by W. E. Vine. It is a work of considerable scholarship, and is recommended for every serious Bible student. Besides giving the meaning of Bible words, Vine often also makes very helpful theological and doctrinal comments about them.

The words in the Dictionary are given as they appear in the Authorized ("King James") Version and the Revised Version of the Bible. It is important to have a copy of one of these Bibles if you are to make full use of Vine's Expository Dictionary. This is because in the more recent translations some of the words are not as they occur in the Authorized and Revised Versions, and so do not appear in the Dictionary.

You may also wish to use the Lexicon at the back of the Dictionary. There the original Greek words are shown in anglicized forms. Under each anglicized Greek word is a list of the ways the word is translated into English. So, for example, the Greek word "doxa" in the Lexicon can be found in the main body of the Dictionary under "dignity," "glory," "honour," "praise," "worship."

By studying a word in this way, you can get a much broader understanding of its use and meaning in the New Testament.

SUGGESTION 3
Bibliography

Below is a brief bibliography of reference books which will help you to deepen your Bible study (commentaries on individual books of the Bible are omitted because of lack of space):

The Amplified Bible (Zondervan)

Bauer, W. (& al.) — *A Greek-English Lexicon of the New Testament and Other Early Christian Literature* (Chicago)

Bruce, F. F. — *New Testament History* (Doubleday)

Douglas, J. D. (& al.) — *New Bible Dictionary* (Tyndale)

Fee, G. & Stewart, D. — *How to Read the Bible For All Its Worth* (Zondervan)

Guthrie, D. (& al.) — *The Eerdmans Bible Commentary* (Eerdmans)

Guthrie, D. — *New Testament Introduction* (IVP)

Marshall, A.	*Interlinear Greek-English New Testament* (Zondervan)
Strong, J.	*Exhaustive Concordance to the Bible* (Nelson)
Throckmorton, B. H.	*Gospel Parallels: A Synopsis of the First Three Gospels* (Nelson)
Vine, W. E.	*An Expository Dictionary of Bible Words* (Bethany House)
Walvoord, J.F. & Zuck, R. B.	*The Bible Knowledge Commentary* (Victor)
Wieand, A. C.	*A New Harmony of the Gospels* (Eerdmans)
Young, R.	*Analytical Concordance to the Holy Bible* (Eerdmans)

PART 4

FORMING AND
LEADING A
BIBLE STUDY GROUP

Forming and Leading
a Bible Study Group

Why Form a Bible Study Discussion Group?
Sometimes Bible study preparation is difficult to sustain. Being part of a discussion group can be a great stimulus to persevere because:

1. You can learn from what others have discovered.
2. You can pass on to others what you have learned.
3. The discussion group times provide a deadline by which to complete your preparation.
4. The group members can pray for one another as they seek to put into practice what they are learning from God.
5. Christian fellowship, especially when centered on the Scriptures, can be a great encouragement and stimulus (Hebrews 10:24,25).

How Do I Go About Setting up a Group?
Ask friends who want to study the Scriptures to join you. Set a regular time to meet, a location and a time by which you will finish the discussion.

It is important that you all agree:
1. to study the same portion of Scripture,
2. in advance,

3. preferably using the same techniques of study,
4. and to attend the group discussion faithfully
5. to discuss what you have learned,
6. to learn from what others share, and
7. to pray for one another at other times.

What About My Own Preparation?

It is very important that the leader should thoroughly study the relevant passage before the group meets. This sets a good example to the other members, and helps the leader to be properly prepared to co-ordinate the discussion.

What Do I Do When the Group Meets?

Set a relaxed, informal atmosphere -- perhaps start with coffee and cake.

Your job as a Bible study group leader is...

1. To be a co-ordinator of the discussion, not a theological expert, nor the one who does all the speaking.
2. To give each one in the group the opportunity to express what he has learned from his study (as well, of course, as participating in the discussion yourself).
3. To promote a courteous, stimulating and relaxed discussion about subjects relevant to what you are studying.
4. To give the group members the opportunity to raise questions about matters they do not understand, or about which they would like to hear the views of others.
5. To stimulate discussion about parts of the chapter which have not been discussed.
6. To summarize the discussion or aspects of it (or invite others to do so).

7. To encourage group members to say how they hope to put into practice what they have been learning.

How Do I Do It?

The key to leading a stimulating discussion group lies in the art of asking questions that promote discussion and encourage participation by the whole group.

Your questions should be the starting point for discussion, not a kind of cross-examination. Ask questions that encourage each person to share with the group what they have learned and how God has spoken to them. After one person has spoken, invite others in the group to comment or ask questions. Try not to ask questions which may pressurize or embarrass people.

Below are some examples of good questions -- and also some bad ones. Why do you think they are good or bad?

- "Do any of you have any questions about what Luke has just said?"

- "Could I perhaps say how I understand this chapter? I think I see it differently from you, Jude."

- "Bartholomew, could you please clarify what you meant by 'eschatological' in that last comment, please?"

- "Have you been too busy again to prepare the Bible study, Judas?"

- "Would someone like to summarize what we have
  said on this subject, please?"

- "Would someone like to start by telling us the main
  thing they learned from this passage?"

- "Does anyone have any suggestions for an outline of
  this chapter?"

- "You're wrong, Peter. Verse 6 doesn't mean that
  at all. Anyone can see that."

- "What are you going to do about this, Thomas?"

- "I'm not sure I know the answer to your question,
  James. Does anyone have any suggestions?"

- "Would someone like to comment on what Matthew
  has just said?"

- "What do you think are the practical implications of
  this teaching?"

How Do I Prepare in Advance?

Until you are confident that you can lead a stimulating
discussion, it may be as well to prepare a few discussion
questions before the meeting. The guidelines below may
help you to do that.

<u>Opening Questions</u>
Make sure your early questions are broad and open-
ended, so that each person can say in a general way what
he has learned from his study and how he has understood the chapter. For example:
    - "What stands out to you from this week's chapter?"
    - "Is there an aspect of this chapter you would like us
      all to discuss?"

Invitation Questions

These are questions which invite others to state what they have learned. For example:
- "Would anyone like to say what they think the writer meant in this verse?"

Commenting Questions

Some questions can stimulate the group members to comment on what has just been said. For example:
- "Does anyone want to add to that?"
- "Are there any comments about what John has said?"

Exploratory Questions

Some questions can promote thought and discussion about an aspect of the chapter not previously discussed. For example:
- "What do we think are the implications of verse 19?"
- "Has anyone given thought to Paul's teaching about honesty in this chapter?"

Application Questions

These are questions which gently encourage the group members to say how God has been challenging them personally, and what they hope to do about it. For example:
- "Would anyone like to say what they hope to do as a result of this study?"
- "Is there something you would like to do about what you have just said?"

Summary Questions

Lastly, some questions can help summarize the group's discussion and its conclusions. For example:
- "How would you summarize what we have said?"

For further practice at identifying types of question, re-read the questions in the "How Do I Do It?" section above and analyse them according to their type.

A Final Word

Leading Bible study discussion groups can be very rewarding and stimulating. After having read these notes, you may feel it is a complicated task! A little practice can take away much of your apprehension. Keep going -- it will be worth it!

> *"My son, do not forget my teaching,*
> *but keep my commands in your heart,*
> *for they will prolong your life many years,*
> *and bring you prosperity.*
> *Let love and faithfulness never leave you;*
> *bind them about your neck,*
> *write them on the tablet of your heart.*
> *Then you will win favour and a good name*
> *in the sight of God and man.*
> *Trust in the Lord with all your heart*
> *and lean not on your own understanding;*
> *in all your ways acknowledge Him,*
> *and he will make your paths straight.*
> *Do not be wise in your own eyes;*
> *fear the Lord and shun evil."*
> (Proverbs 3:1-7)